D1451113

BEYOND
PASTA

Project Editor: Lisa M. Tooker
Translator: Christie Tam
Editor: Lynda Zuber Sassi
Design & Typography: Elizabeth M. Watson
Layout & Production: Patty Holden
Photography & Recipes: Teubner Foodfoto JmbH

Printed in China

ISBN: 1-59637-020-3

CONTENTS

SPAGHETTI

LASAGNE

RAVIOLI

INTRODUCTION

WHERE PASTA ORIGINATED IS NOT EXACTLY CLEAR. It is on record that the Chinese ate pasta as early as 5,000 BC. Some think that Marco Polo brought pasta to Italy in 1279, and that Thomas Jefferson is responsible for its proliferation throughout the United States. One thing that is certain is today, pasta is equally important in Asia, Italy, and the United States.

Despite fad diets and carbohydrate counting, pasta's popularity in the United States continues to prosper. Whether as a first course, a main course, or the only course, pasta has become America's comfort food. In fact, on average, Americans eat 20 pounds of pasta per year. Our counterparts in Italy eat 65 pounds a year!

Pasta comes in all shapes, sizes, and flavors. Part of the beauty of pasta is that it's quick, it's easy, and it's affordable. It's also versatile and perfect for improvising. Look in the refrigerator or pantry and you are sure to find something that can be tossed into pasta and served for tonight's dinner.

THIS BOOK IS DIVIDED INTO CHAPTERS BASED ON PASTA TYPE. There are noodles and tubes, stuffed pastas, lasagne (which is really any pasta baked in a pan), and gnocchi (which aren't really pasta at all). Our recipes can either be made with fresh, homemade pasta or dry pasta from the store. General instructions that apply to the recipes throughout this book are outlined below.

Mangiamo!

TUBES

RIBBONS

GNOCCHI

PASTA BASICS

QUALITY

When purchasing pasta instead of making it at home, be sure to buy the best quality. Look for pasta that is made of 100 percent durum wheat. Brands we like that are readily available include De Cecco and Barillo. Other fancy Italian or American brands are fine too; the key is the ingredients. Although some high-quality, fresh pasta is available, it probably won't compete with what you make at home. So if you don't have time to make it and aren't sure of the freshness, then try a dry pasta instead. Because, fresh or dry, top-quality pasta tastes better, is easier to keep from overcooking, and has a texture that helps the sauce to stick.

COOKING TO AL DENTE

The rule of thumb is for every pound of pasta, you need at least five quarts of water. Bring the water to an aggressive boil and add a couple tablespoons of kosher salt. Contrary to what you may have learned before, there is no need to add oil to the water. Add the pasta and stir so it doesn't stick. Bring the water back to a boil and stir every minute or two. Ample water and frequent stirring minimize sticking. All pasta in this book should be cooked until al dente (al-DEN-tay) literally meaning "to the tooth," which is how to test pasta to see if it is properly cooked. The pasta should be a bit firm, offering some resistance to the tooth, but tender. The cooking times will vary. The best way to check is to taste the pasta as it is cooking. If you're using dry pasta, consult with the package directions for cooking times.

DRAINING

Once the pasta has been cooked to al dente, it needs to be drained. Pour it into a colander and then put it in a warm bowl. It is important that the bowl is warm, as this will keep the pasta warm. There will still be some water on the pasta; it doesn't need to be dry. Whatever you do, do not rinse the pasta with cold water. This will make it cold and strip some flavor. Since pasta cooks relatively quickly, unless noted in the recipe, it is best to make the sauce ahead of time so it is ready when the pasta is done cooking.

SAUCING

And speaking of saucing, Americans are notorious for over-saucing. Pasta should not drown in its sauce, just as the sauce should not clump onto the pasta. The goal is to have a sauce that evenly coats and compliments. So, if your pasta is drowning, add more pasta, or pour less sauce. Alternately, if you find yourself with a sauce deficit, add a little of the cooking water (the Italians do) and thin the sauce until it becomes a better consistency.

CHEESE

Cheese, pasta, and olive oil—an Italian triumvirate. The key to the cheese, like the pasta, is that it is top-quality. Two of the cheeses that you will find throughout this book are Parmigiano-Reggiano and Pecorino.

Parmigiano-Reggiano is a hard cheese made with cow's milk from the region around Parma, Italy. Any other cheese claiming to be Parmesan is an imposter! Little compares to freshly grated Parmigiano-Reggiano. It's a cheese with incomparable flavor, texture, and richness. In addition to enhancing the flavor of many types of pasta, it is also wonderful as a table cheese and can be eaten on its own. Parmigiano-Reggiano lasts a long time in the refrigerator, and though expensive, it is worth every penny.

Pecorino, Pecorino Romano, and Pecorino Sardo is hard cheese made from sheep's milk. Pecorino has a stronger, sharper flavor than Parmigiano-Reggiano and is best grated atop pastas that are richer and more robust. Pecorino is also divine to nibble on its own, on a slice of crusty baguette with a little olive oil drizzled on top.

PORTIONS

Generally speaking, one pound of pasta will serve six to eight people for a small, first course, or three to four people for a main course. If your sauce is hearty and you're also serving bread, meat, vegetables, and a salad, of course, the pasta will go far. However, if all you're having is pasta with bread or salad, and you're feeding hungry people, one pound could be consumed by two! So, think of your audience and what else you're feeding them and prepare proportions accordingly. Most recipes in this book are meant to serve four people a dinner-sized portion.

SPAGHETTI

SPAGHETTI IS PROBABLY THE BEST KNOWN of all pasta types. It is extremly versatile. Spaghetti and meatballs is an American invention. Italians used to eat meat only a few times a month. When they came to America, where meat was more plentiful, they started to incorporate it into their spaghetti. In this chapter, spaghetti is our pasta of choice. However, feel free to experiment and substitute other members of the family, spaghettini (thin spaghetti), linguini (flat), capellini (fine angel hair), and bucatini (with a hole in the middle like a drinking straw).

Spaghetti with Tomatoes and Mozzarella

16 oz spaghetti
28 oz diced tomatoes
1 small yellow onion, diced
1 red chile pepper, seeded and
    cut into strips
1 tbs basil, cut into strips
⅓ cup extra virgin olive oil
7 oz buffalo mozzarella
Kosher salt
Freshly ground pepper

IN A LARGE POT, cook spaghetti in boiling, salted water according to package directions until al dente and drain.

IN A BOWL, combine tomatoes, onions, chile pepper, salt, pepper, basil, and olive oil. Drain mozzarella and cut into 1 inch cubes. Toss spaghetti with the tomatoes. Add mozzarella and serve immediately.

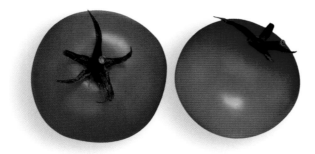

Spaghetti with Tomato-Eggplant Sauce

3 tbs olive oil
1 small yellow onion, chopped
2 cloves garlic
⅔ cup eggplant, diced
28 oz diced tomatoes
1 tbs tomato paste
Pinch of cayenne pepper
1 tbs chopped parsley
16 oz spaghetti
3 tbs grated Parmigiano-Reggiano
Kosher salt
Freshly ground pepper

IN A SAUCEPAN, heat olive oil and sauté onions and garlic until translucent. Add the eggplant, tomatoes and tomato paste, and cook for 2–3 minutes. Add cayenne pepper and season to taste with salt and pepper. Simmer gently for 10–15 minutes. Sprinkle in parsley and remove from heat.

COOK SPAGHETTI in boiling, salted water according to package directions until al dente and drain. Add the spaghetti to the pan and combine with sauce, over low heat 2–3 minutes until warm.

TO SERVE: Divide pasta onto warm plates and sprinkle top of spaghetti with Parmigiano-Reggiano.

Spaghetti with Olives and Anchovies

4 anchovy fillets in brine
¼ cup extra virgin olive oil
2 cloves garlic, minced
¼ cup onions, chopped
28 oz diced tomatoes
½ cup pitted black olives, chopped
2 tbs salt-packed capers, rinsed
2 tbs chopped parsley
16 oz spaghetti
Kosher salt
Freshly ground pepper

RINSE ANCHOVIES, pat dry, and chop finely. In a saucepan, heat olive oil and sauté garlic and onions until translucent. Add tomatoes, reduce heat, and simmer for 15 minutes, stirring occasionally. Add anchovies, olives, capers, and parsley. Stir well and season to taste with salt and pepper.

COOK SPAGHETTI in boiling, salted water according to package directions until al dente and drain.

TO SERVE: Divide spaghetti onto warm plates and top with sauce.

Spaghetti with Basil Pesto

1 cup basil leaves
3 cloves garlic, peeled
3 tbs pine nuts
3½ oz freshly grated
    Parmigiano-Reggiano
¾ cup olive oil
16 oz spaghetti
Basil leaves and pine nuts
    for garnish
Kosher salt
Freshly ground pepper

IN A BLENDER OR FOOD PROCESSOR, combine basil, garlic, and pine nuts. Process into a paste and transfer to a bowl. Stir in Parmigiano-Reggiano and add olive oil one drop at a time, stirring until absorbed into the paste. Season to taste with salt and pepper.

COOK SPAGHETTI IN BOILING, salted water according to package directions until al dente and drain.

TO SERVE: Toss spaghetti and pesto together and garnish with additional basil leaves and pine nuts.

THIS SAUCE is easy to prepare in advance and keeps in a sealed jar in the refrigerator for up to three weeks.

TIP

► This sauce is easy to prepare in advance and keeps in a sealed jar in the refrigerator for up to three weeks.

Spaghetti alla Bolognese

⅓ cup butter
¼ cup onions, chopped
¼ cup carrots, diced
¼ cup celery, diced
¾ lb lean ground beef
½ cup beef stock
8 oz diced tomatoes
2 tbs tomato paste
1 tbs chopped parsley
1 tsp chopped thyme
1 tsp chopped basil
½ cup red wine
16 oz spaghetti
⅓ cup Parmigiano-
    Reggiano, grated
Kosher salt
Freshly ground pepper

IN A LARGE SAUCEPAN, melt butter and sauté onions, carrots, and celery. Increase the heat and brown the ground beef. Add stock, tomatoes, tomato paste, parsley, thyme, and basil. Season to taste with salt and pepper. Bring to a boil, reduce heat, cover, and simmer for 40–50 minutes. Add wine and let simmer for another 10 minutes.

COOK SPAGHETTI in boiling, salted water according to package directions until al dente and drain.

TO SERVE: Divide spaghetti onto warm plates, top with sauce, and sprinkle over top of spaghetti with Parmigiano-Reggiano.

Spaghetti all' Arabiata

2 tbs olive oil
1 oz smoked bacon
2 tbs onions, chopped
2 tbs shallots, chopped
1 clove garlic, minced
2 tbs celery, chopped
2 whole cloves
2 tbs tomato paste
15 oz diced tomatoes
2 tsp red pepper flakes
1 bay leaf
2 sprigs thyme
1 small sprig rosemary
16 oz spaghetti
½ cup Parmigiano-
    Reggiano, grated
Basil for garnish
Kosher salt
Freshly ground pepper

IN A SAUCEPAN, heat olive oil and cook bacon until crispy. Stir in onions, shallots, garlic, celery, and cloves. Add tomato paste and sauté over moderate heat for 10 minutes. Strain and add the tomatoes, red pepper flakes, bay leaf, thyme, and rosemary. Season to taste with salt and pepper. Reduce heat and simmer for 35–40 minutes. Remove bay leaf, thyme, and rosemary. Set aside sauce in saucepan.

COOK SPAGHETTI in boiling, salted water according to package directions until al dente and drain.

TO SERVE: Toss spaghetti with sauce and sprinkle with a little Parmigiano-Reggiano and garnish with additional basil.

Spaghetti with Tomato Sauce

2 tbs vegetable oil
2 tbs minced onions
8 oz diced tomatoes
8 oz whole tomatoes
16 oz spaghetti
Kosher salt
Freshly ground pepper

IN A SAUCEPAN, heat oil and sauté onions until translucent. Add tomatoes and simmer for 10 minutes. Season to taste with salt and pepper.

COOK SPAGHETTI in boiling, salted water according to package directions until al dente and drain.

TO SERVE: Divide spaghetti onto warm plates and top with tomato sauce.

TIP

▶ For a variation with meatballs, here's a favorite to share with the whole family, Spaghetti and Meatballs. In a bowl, add ⅓ lb ground beef, 2 tbs minced onions, 2 tbs diced green bell peppers with seeds removed, 1 egg yolk, 2 tbs bread crumbs, pinch of Hungarian sweet paprika, and 1 tbs chopped parsley. Season to taste with salt and pepper. Shape into 12 small meatballs. In a pan, heat 2 tbs of oil and saute meatballs on all sides for 4–5 mintues. Follow recipe above for tomato sauce and add meatballs to the sauce. Follow directions above for cooking spaghetti and serving.

LASAGNE

IT IS THOUGHT AMONGST SCHOLARS that lasagne is the original dried pasta. It dates back to the 14th century, or before in some books. The Italian word lasagne refers to a dish that's cooked in a pot. Literally speaking, all of the recipes in this chapter are lasagne, even though we may know them with different names today. They are all baked in some form of casserole dish with layers of pasta surrounded by supporting ingredients.

Lasagne Verdi

10 oz chopped spinach
3 tbs bread crumbs
¼ cup pecorino cheese, grated
Pinch of freshly grated nutmeg
2 cups eggplant, sliced
1¾ cups zucchini, sliced
⅓ cup flour
3 eggs
2 tbs vegetable oil, separated
1 clove garlic, minced
10½ oz porcini mushrooms,
    cleaned and sliced
1 tbs chopped parsley
3 eggs
½ cup pecorino cheese, grated
¼ cup heavy cream
16 oz lasagne noodles
28 oz tomato sauce
⅔ cup fontina cheese, cubed
Kosher salt
Freshly ground pepper

IN A BOWL, combine spinach, bread crumbs, pecorino, nutmeg, salt, and pepper. Set aside.

SPRINKLE EGGPLANT AND ZUCCHINI with salt and pepper. Sift flour onto a plate. Whisk eggs in a shallow bowl. One by one, dredge eggplant and zucchini slices in eggs then flour (shaking off excess). In a pan, heat 1 tablespoon of oil and fry vegetables in batches for 1 minute on each side. Place on paper towels. In a separate pan, heat remaining oil and sauté garlic until translucent. Add mushrooms and parsley, season with salt and pepper, and cook 1–2 minutes, tossing occasionally. Remove mushrooms from heat and set aside.

IN A BOWL, combine the eggs, pecorino, cream, and season with salt and pepper.

MEANWHILE, cook the lasagne noodles according to package directions. Remove, drain, and set aside unitl ready to assemble lasagne.

PREHEAT OVEN TO 350°F. In a 9 by 13 inch casserole dish, spread half the tomato sauce evenly over the bottom. Place lasagne noodles on top to cover, followed by a layer of eggplant. Top evenly with spinach. Pour half the cream sauce over the spinach. Place a second row of lasagne noodles in the dish, followed by a layer of zucchini. Top evenly with mushrooms, cover with remaining tomato sauce, and a third layer of lasagne noodles. Cut fontina into small cubes, place on top of the lasagne noodles, and cover with remaining cream sauce. Bake for 20–25 minutes.

Pastitsío

¾ lb eggplant
2 cloves garlic, minced
½ cup plus 2 tbs vegetable
    oil, separated
6 cups veal stock
12 oz ziti macaroni
1 small chile pepper, seeds removed
    and chopped finely
5 oz smoked bacon, diced
¼ cup onions, peeled and diced
3 tbs carrots, diced
¼ cup leeks, white parts only, diced
1⅓ lb cubed lamb
2 cups tomatoes, diced
1 tbs chopped thyme
1 tbs chopped parsley
2 tbs butter
2 tbs flour
1 cup milk
¼ cup Kefalotyri, grated
Kosher salt
Freshly ground pepper

PREPARE THE EGGPLANT: Cut into ¼ inch slices. Arrange by layering eggplant slices in a container, adding garlic, pouring ½ cup oil over the top, and seasoning with salt and pepper. Cover and marinate for at least 1 hour.

IN A LARGE POT, bring veal stock to a boil. Add macaroni and cook according to package directions until al dente. Drain (saving the stock), cover, and set aside. Pour stock back into the pot and slowly reduce to about ½ cup.

SEASON LAMB with chile pepper, salt, and pepper. In a saucepan, heat 2 tablespoons remaining oil and sauté bacon, onions, carrots, and leeks. Add lamb and brown for several minutes, stirring. Add tomatoes and cook for another 5–10 minutes. Add reduced stock, thyme, and parsley. Continue cooking uncovered until the liquid has almost evaporated.

PREHEAT OVEN TO 400°F. In a pan, melt butter and add flour. Stir in milk until smooth, season with salt and pepper, and boil for about 20 minutes, stirring. Add Kefalotyri and melt. Butter a 9 by 13 inch baking dish, fill as shown, and bake for 30–40 minutes.

Fazzoletti with Scallops

2 tbs butter, separated
1 clove garlic, minced
1 tbs shallots, minced
12 oz chopped spinach
10 medium scallops
2 tbs vegetable oil, separated
⅓ cup celery, chopped
1 leek, white part only, chopped
1 carrot, chopped
¾ cup fish stock
½ cup heavy cream
1 tsp lemon juice
16 oz lasagne noodles
¼ cup Parmigiano-
    Reggiano, grated
Kosher salt
Freshly ground pepper

IN A SAUCEPAN, melt 1 tablespoon of butter and sauté garlic and shallots until translucent. Add spinach, toss, and season with salt and pepper. Cover and set aside.

CUT SCALLOPS into ½ inch pieces. In a pan, heat 1 tablespoon oil and sear scallops briefly. Remove and set aside.

IN THE SAME PAN, heat remaining oil and cook celery, leek, and carrot for about 2 minutes. Add scallops, and season with salt and pepper. Set aside.

IN A PAN, combine fish stock and cream and bring to a boil. Reduce to a simmer and season with lemon juice, salt, and pepper.

COOK LASAGNE NOODLES in boiling, salted water according to package directions until al dente. Remove, drain, and cut into 4 by 2 inch pieces.

TO ASSEMBLE: Place 1 lasagne noodle on each plate and cover with a layer of spinach. Top with another noodle and scallops. Finish with a third noodle. Pour sauce over the top, sprinkle with Parmigiano-Reggiano, and heat under the broiler for about 5 minutes. Serve immediately.

Baked Penne
with Camembert

16 oz penne pasta
3 tbs vegetable oil
3 tbs green onions, chopped
    into rings
½ cup zucchini, sliced
½ cup red bell peppers, seeds
    removed and sliced
1 cup cooked ham, cubed
1 tbs chopped parsley
Pinch of Hungarian sweet paprika
10 oz Camembert
3 eggs
½ cup heavy cream
½ cup milk
Several basil leaves for garnish
Kosher salt
Freshly ground pepper

COOK PENNE IN BOILING, salted water according to package directions until al dente. Drain.

IN A LARGE PAN, heat oil and sauté onions, zucchini, and bell peppers for 2–3 minutes. Add ham and sauté briefly. Toss with penne and parsley, and season to taste with paprika, salt, and pepper. Remove rind from Camembert and cut into ¼ inch cubes.

PREHEAT OVEN TO 375°F. Transfer half the pasta to a lightly-oiled casserole dish. Sprinkle half the Camembert over the top. Cover with remaining pasta and a second layer of Camembert.

IN A BOWL, whisk together eggs, cream, and milk. Season to taste with salt and pepper and pour over the casserole. Bake for 35–40 minutes. Garnish with basil leaves and serve.

Lasagne al Forno

3 tbs vegetable oil
1 clove garlic, minced
⅓ cup onions, chopped
1⅓ lb ground beef
1 bay leaf
1–2 cups beef stock
28 oz peeled tomatoes
1 tbs chopped parsley
16 oz lasagne noodles
2 tbs butter
2 tbs flour
2 cups milk
Freshly grated nutmeg
2 balls mozzarella di bufala,
   drained and sliced
⅓ cup Parmigiano-
   Reggiano, grated
Kosher salt
Freshly ground pepper

IN A PAN, heat oil, add garlic and onions, and sauté until translucent. Add beef and brown until crumbly. Add bay leaf, 1 cup stock, tomatoes, and season with salt and pepper. Bring to a boil. If the sauce gets too thick, add more stock. Reduce heat to low and add parsley.

COOK LASAGNE NOODLES according to package directions until al dente, drain, and arrange side by side on a towel.

IN A SAUCEPAN, heat butter and add flour to form a blond roux. Add milk and whisk vigorously. Reduce heat and simmer for about 10 minutes. Season to taste with nutmeg, salt, and pepper.

PREHEAT OVEN TO 350°F. Brush a baking dish with oil and line the bottom with a layer of lasagne noodles. Add one third of the ground beef and one third of the sauce. Top with one third of the mozzarella, season with pepper, and top with one third of the Parmigiano-Reggiano. Repeat this process until all the ingredients have been used, finishing with sauce and Parmigiano-Reggiano on top layer.

BAKE in the oven on the middle rack for 30–40 minutes.

Shrimp Stuffed Shells

3 tbs vegetable oil
3 tbs shallots, peeled and minced
3 tbs green onions, sliced
1⅓ cups sauerkraut
⅓ cup pineapple chunks, drained
Pinch cayenne pepper
½ cup Prosecco
5 oz cooked shrimp, chopped
1 tsp chopped sage
16 oz conchiglioni pasta
3 tbs butter
1 tbs chopped parsley
Kosher salt
Freshly ground pepper

IN A PAN, heat oil, add shallots and sauté until translucent then add onions, sauerkraut, and pineapple. Season with cayenne, salt, and pepper. Add Prosecco and simmer for 5–6 minutes. Stir in shrimp and add sage. Simmer for 5–6 more minutes.

COOK CONCHIGLIONI in boiling, salted water according to package directions until al dente and drain. Let cool slightly.

PREHEAT OVEN TO 400°F. Butter a casserole dish. Stuff shells with shrimp filling and place in the casserole dish. Bake for 20 minutes. (If shells begin to brown, cover with foil.)

TO SERVE: Sprinkle with parsley and dip in a sweet, hot chili sauce.

Cannelloni Stuffed with Oyster Mushrooms

1⅓ cups oyster mushrooms
¼ cup butter
⅓ cup onions
2 garlic cloves, peeled and minced
¾ lb lean ground pork
1¾ cups fresh spinach

Béchamel sauce
2 tbs butter
1 tbs flour
⅔ cup milk

8 cannelloni shells
15 oz tomato sauce
2 tbs grated Parmigiano-Reggiano
Kosher salt
Freshly ground pepper

SEPARATE MUSHROOMS, clean, and cut into strips. In a pan, melt butter and sauté onions and garlic until translucent. Add pork and brown until crumbly. Add spinach and mushrooms, sauté briefly, season with salt and pepper, and set aside.

MAKE THE BÉCHAMEL SAUCE: In a saucepan, heat butter, stir in flour, and sauté to form a blond roux. Add milk, stir until smooth, and bring to a boil. Reduce the heat, season with salt and pepper, and simmer for 20 minutes, stirring.

COOK CANNELLONI SHELLS in boiling, salted water according to package directions. Run cold water over them and lay out on damp kitchen towels.

PREHEAT OVEN TO 400°F. Fill cannelloni shells with mushroom filling. Pour half the tomato sauce into a casserole dish then arrange cannelloni, side-by-side. Pour remaining tomato sauce and béchamel sauce over the top. Sprinkle Parmigiano-Reggiano and bake for 20–25 minutes, until golden-brown.

Pasta Pie with Shrimp and Vegetables

1 (9 inch) prepared pie
    dough, thawed
1 egg yolk
8 oz spaghetti
2 tbs butter
¼ cup white onions, chopped
1 garlic clove, minced
½ cup carrots, peeled and diced
½ cup celery, sliced diagonally
¼ cup white wine
⅓ cup frozen peas, thawed
⅓ lb raw, peeled shrimp
¾ cup heavy cream
3 eggs
¼ cup Parmigiano-
    Reggiano, grated
Kosher salt
Freshly ground pepper

PREHEAT OVEN TO 400°F. Line a round baking dish with pie dough. Pinch together sides and brush with egg yolk. Score the bottom of the dough and line with parchment paper. Bake for 20 minutes. Remove from oven and remove parchment, and cool slightly.

COOK SPAGHETTI in boiling, salted water according to package directions until al dente and drain.

IN A PAN, melt butter and sauté onions and garlic until translucent. Add carrots, celery, wine, and season with salt and pepper. Cover, reduce heat, and cook for 5 minutes. Add peas and cook for 5 minutes. Finally, add shrimp and cook 2–3 more minutes. Stir in spaghetti, season with salt and pepper, and remove from heat.

IN A BOWL, whisk together cream and eggs, and season with salt and pepper. Fill pie dough with spaghetti and cover with cream. Sprinkle the top with Parmigiano-Reggiano and bake for 25–30 minutes.

RAVIOLI

SINCE PASTA DOUGH is relatively benign in flavor, the options for stuffed pasta are endless. When making stuffed pasta, think like an Italian, if the filling is complex in flavor, the sauce should be simple, and if the sauce is complex in flavor, stick with a simple filling. In this chapter, we focus mostly on ravioli. Experiment with our Basic Stuffed Pasta Dough recipe (page 44) by making different stuffed pasta shapes such as tortellini and agnolotti as well as by stuffing dried pasta like conchiglie, manicotti, and cannelloni.

Basic Stuffed

Pasta Dough

½ cup durum wheat semolina
½ cup white flour
2 eggs
1 egg yolk
⅓ tsp salt
A little water as needed

HEAP SEMOLINA AND FLOUR on a work surface and form a well in the center. Place eggs, egg yolk, and salt in the well and stir with a spoon, gradually working in more flour from around the edges. Using both hands, push flour from the outside toward the center and gradually work in. Knead into a smooth, elastic dough (takes about 10 minutes). Wrap in plastic wrap and refrigerate for 1 hour.

FOR INSTRUCTIONS on rolling out and cutting pasta see pages 64–65.

TIP

► Raviolis are easy to freeze. Line them up on a rack in the freezer overnight and then pack them in airtight bags or containers.

1. Place eggs and egg yolk in center of well.

2. Using a spoon, stir mixture.

3. Use both hands to push flour to center.

4. Knead dough.

5. Continue kneading dough for 10 minutes.

6. Dough will be smooth when done.

7. Wrap in plastic.

Salmon Ravioli with Bell Pepper Sauce

5 oz skinless salmon fillet
½ cup heavy cream, separated
2 tbs green onions, chopped
Dash of lime juice
Pinch of cayenne pepper

Sauce
1 tbs chopped dill
2 tbs butter
2 tbs minced shallots
1 clove garlic, minced
2 cups red bell peppers, seeds
   removed and diced
½ red chile pepper, seeds
   removed and diced
1 sprig thyme
1 bay leaf
¼ cup white wine
⅔ cup fish stock

Ravioli
Basic Stuffed Pasta Dough
   (recipe on page 44)
1 egg yolk, whisked
3 tbs grated Parmigiano-Reggiano
Kosher salt
Freshly ground pepper

MAKE THE FILLING: In a blender, purée salmon, ⅓ cup cream, green onions, lime juice, cayenne, and dill. Season with salt and pepper and refrigerate.

MAKE THE SAUCE: In a saucepan melt the butter. Add shallots and garlic and sauté until translucent. Add bell peppers and chile pepper and cook until they begin to soften. Add thyme, bay leaf, wine and stock, and simmer over low heat. When the sauce has been reduced by half, add remaining cream, reduce slightly, then remove thyme, and bay leaf. Purée with a hand blender and put through a fine strainer. Season the sauce to taste with salt and pepper.

MAKE THE RAVIOLI: Roll dough out into a thin sheet. Using a scalloped cookie cutter, cut out circles with a 3 inch diameter. Remove excess dough around the edges and roll out again. Place 1 teaspoon of the filling in the center of each circle. Brush the edges with a little egg yolk. Fold dough over the filling to form semicircular pockets and press edges together tightly.

COOK RAVIOLI in boiling, salted water for about 8 minutes, remove, and let drain.

TO SERVE: Divide ravioli onto plates and pour sauce over the top. Garnish with Parmigiano-Reggiano.

Ravioli with Sage Butter

2 tbs butter, separated
2 shallots, diced
½ cup cooked ham, diced
⅔ cup sour cream
¼ cup lime juice
Zest from 1 lime
2 eggs, 1 separated
½ cup Parmigiano-
    Reggiano, grated
1 tbs bread crumbs
Basic Stuffed Pasta Dough
    (recipe on page 44)
1 tbs chopped sage
Kosher salt
Freshly ground pepper

IN A PAN, heat 1 tablespoon of butter and sauté shallots until translucent. Stir in ham, remove from heat, and let cool. In a bowl, stir sour cream until smooth then combine ham, lime juice, lime zest, egg yolk, egg, Parmigiano-Reggiano, and bread crumbs. Season to taste with salt and pepper.

ROLL DOUGH OUT into a thin sheet. Using a scalloped cookie cutter, cut out circles with a 3 inch diameter. Remove excess dough around the edges and roll out again. Place 1 teaspoon of the filling in the center of each circle. Brush the edges with a little egg white. Fold dough over the filling to form semicircular pockets and press edges together tightly.

COOK IN BATCHES in boiling, salted water for 4–5 minutes. Remove with a slotted spoon and drain.

HEAT SAGE AND REMAINING BUTTER until foamy. Pour over ravioli and toss with Parmigiano-Reggiano.

Deep-Fried Ricotta Pockets

⅔ cup ricotta cheese
2 oz air-dried ham (Parma or
    San Daniele), cubed
¼ cup pecorino cheese, grated
2 tbs green onions, sliced into
    small rings
1 tbs chopped parsley
Pinch of Hungarian sweet paprika
1 egg, separated
15 oz diced tomatoes
¼ cup carrots, diced
¼ cup onions, diced
¼ cup celery, diced
Basic Stuffed Pasta Dough
    (recipe on page 44)
Vegetable oil for deep-frying
Basil for garnish
Kosher salt
Freshly ground pepper

IN A BOWL, combine ricotta, ham, pecorino, onions, parsley, paprika, and egg yolk. Stir together and season generously with salt and pepper.

IN A POT, combine tomatoes, carrots, onions, and celery. Cover, and simmer over low heat for 40 minutes until tender. Season mixture with salt and pepper.

ROLL DOUGH OUT into a thin sheet. Using a scalloped cookie cutter, cut out circles with a 4 inch diameter. Remove excess dough around the edges and roll out again. Place 1 teaspoon of the filling in the center of each circle. Brush the edges with a little egg white. Fold dough over the filling to form semicircular pockets and press edges together tightly.

IN A DEEP-FRYER OR LARGE PAN, heat vegetable oil to 350°F. Fry ricotta pockets until golden. Remove with a slotted spoon and drain thoroughly on paper towels.

TO SERVE: Divide onto plates, pour sauce over the top, and garnish with basil.

MAKES ABOUT 24

Mushroom Ravioli

2 oz bacon, cubed
¼ cup onions, chopped
7 oz porcini mushrooms,
    cleaned and diced
2 tbs chopped parsley, separated
Basic Stuffed Pasta Dough
    (recipe on page 44)
1 egg white, whisked
3 tbs olive oil
3 tbs chopped onions
1 clove garlic, minced
1⅓ lb yellow tomatoes, diced
Kosher salt
Freshly ground pepper

IN A SAUCEPAN, sauté bacon until crispy. Add onions and cook until translucent. Add mushrooms and cook for 2–3 more minutes. Add 1 tablespoon parsley and season to taste with salt and pepper.

ROLL DOUGH OUT into a thin sheet. Using a smooth cookie cutter, cut out circles with a 2½ inch diameter. Remove excess dough around the edges and roll out again. Place a little of the filling in the center of each circle. Brush the edges with egg white. Fold dough over the filling to form semicircular pockets and press edges together tightly. Set aside.

IN A SAUCEPAN, heat oil and sauté onions and garlic until translucent. Stir in tomatoes and remaining parsley, and season with salt and pepper. Reduce heat and simmer for 5 minutes.

COOK RAVIOLI in boiling, salted water for 6–8 minutes, remove, and drain.

TO SERVE: Divide ravioli onto plates and drizzle with tomato sauce.

Seafood Ravioli

¾ lb white fish filets (e.g., cod,
     sole, halibut)
1 tbs olive oil
1 tbs lemon juice
3 oz cooked and peeled shrimp,
     chopped
1 cup crème fraîche, separated
⅔ cup ricotta cheese
¼ cup chopped basil, separated
Basic Stuffed Pasta Dough
     (recipe on page 44)
1 egg white, whisked
Kosher salt
Freshly ground pepper

RINSE FISH and pat dry. Place on an oiled sheet of aluminum foil and season with salt and pepper. Drizzle with olive oil and lemon juice. Cover with foil over and steam for 10–12 minutes. In a food processor, combine fish, shrimp, ½ cup crème fraîche, ricotta, and 2 tablespoons basil. Season to taste with salt and pepper.

ROLL DOUGH OUT into a thin sheet. Using a fluted pastry wheel, cut dough into 1½ by 2½ inch rectangles and place a little filling on one half of each. Remove excess dough and roll out again, filling as before. Brush the edges with egg white. Fold pasta dough over the filling and press edges together tightly.

COOK IN BOILING, salted water for 7–8 minutes. Remove raviolis from water with a slotted spoon and drain.

IN THE MEANTIME, heat remaining crème fraîche over low heat and season with salt and pepper. Remove the sauce from burner and stir in remaining basil.

TO SERVE: Arrange ravioli on plates and drizzle with sauce.

Beet-Filled Ravioli

⅔ lb beets
¼ cup butter
1 egg plus 1 egg white
1⅓ cups ricotta cheese
¼ cup bread crumbs
Basic Stuffed Pasta Dough
    (recipe on p. 44)
¼ cup butter
¼ cup Parmigiano-Reggiano
    cheese, grated
Kosher salt
Freshly ground pepper

GENTLY REMOVE ROOTS from beets. Rinse bulbs, place in a pot of water, cover, and boil for 45–60 minutes until tender. Test with a sharp knife to determine if beets are tender all the way through. Remove, plunge into cold water, peel, chop, and purée in a blender.

IN A SAUCEPAN, melt butter. Add beets and cook over low heat for 10 minutes. Season with salt and pepper. Let cool.

IN A BOWL, combine ricotta, 1 egg and bread crumbs, and season with salt and pepper.

ROLL DOUGH OUT into a thin sheet. Using a smooth cookie cutter, cut out circles with a 3 inch diameter. Remove excess dough around the edges and roll out again. Spoon ricotta into the center of each circle and then spoon beet purée on the top. Brush the edges with egg white. Fold dough over the filling to form semicircular pockets and press edges together tightly. Set aside.

COOK RAVIOLI in boiling, salted water for 5–6 minutes. Remove with a slotted spoon and drain.

MELT BUTTER and brown slightly. Arrange ravioli on plates, drizzle with butter, and garnish with Parmigiano-Reggiano.

MAKES 24 RAVIOLI

Turkish Manti

Cornmeal dough
⅔ cup cornmeal
⅔ cup white flour
5 eggs
3 egg yolks
1 tbs olive oil
½ tsp salt
Freshly grated nutmeg

Lamb filling
¼ cup olive oil, separated
¼ cup onions, diced
⅓ cup green onions, diced
1 clove garlic, minced
¼ cup carrots, diced
⅔ lb ground lamb meat
1 small chile pepper, seeds removed
    and diced
1 tbs chopped parsley
1 tbs chopped mint leaves

Sauce
2 cloves garlic, minced
⅔ cup plain yogurt

Kosher salt
Freshly ground pepper

MAKE THE CORNMEAL DOUGH: Combine the cornmeal and flour, heap on a work surface, and form a well in the center. Place eggs, egg yolks, olive oil, salt and nutmeg in the well, and knead into a smooth dough. Wrap in plastic wrap and let stand for 1 hour.

MAKE THE LAMB FILLING: In a pan, heat 3 tablespoons oil and sauté onions and garlic until translucent. Add carrots and cook until tender. Add remaining oil and brown lamb for 4 minutes, then add chile pepper, parsley, and mint. Season to taste with salt and pepper, stirring.

ROLL OUT PASTA DOUGH as thinly as possible and follow the steps shown in the photos.

MAKE THE SAUCE: In a bowl, combine garlic and yogurt and season with salt and pepper.

TO SERVE: Divide manti onto 4 plates and drizzle sauce over the top.

TIP

▶ Manti originated in Anatole, Turkey and as with Italian ravioli, they should be made as small as possible. Cornmeal is added to the dough, which gives it a rustic texture and firmness.

1. Cut a thin sheet of dough into 1½ by 1½ inch squares and place a mound of filling in the center of each.

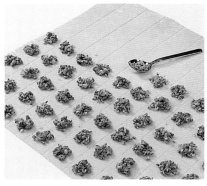

2. Brush edges of dough with water. Press squares together so that all the corners meet at the top center. Press diagonal edges firmly together.

3. Cook in boiling, salted water until they rise to the surface. Remove and drain.

TUBES

TUBE PASTA IS THE PERFECT ACCOMPANIMENT for chunky sauces. This chapter gives you the option to make your own pasta, or use dried pasta from the store. The Basic Pasta Dough recipe can be used for all the recipes, what will differ is the shape in which the pasta is formed. Our basic recipe uses durum wheat semolina, which enables the pasta to dry quickly and be cooked al dente, "to the tooth," tender, but firm.

Basic Pasta Dough

½ cup durum wheat semolina
1¾ cups white flour
5 eggs
1 egg yolk
1 tsp salt
½ tbs oil
Flour for the work surface

Special equipment
Pasta maker

POUR SEMOLINA AND FLOUR onto a work surface and form a well in the center. Place eggs in the well one at a time, followed by the egg yolk. Add salt and oil. Using a fork or spoon, first stir together ingredients in the well, then gradually add semolina, and flour from the edges of the well to form a thick mixture. Using both hands, continue to add flour from the outer edges, combining it with the dough. Press the flour into the dough. If the dough doesn't absorb all the flour (i.e., it is difficult to combine the ingredients), add a little water. Work in water with both thumbs and fold the dough over itself to knead in remaining flour. Now begins the actual kneading. Spread out dough with the heels of your hands, first in one direction, then in another, folding it over onto itself each time to form a smooth, firm dough that retains its shape. Wrap in plastic wrap and let stand for about 1 hour.

DIVIDE DOUGH into 3 parts. Roll out each third on a floured work surface as thinly as possible. Use a pasta maker to roll out the dough to the desired thickness. Using the proper attachment, cut dough into strips or ribbons that are the desired width.

FOR TAGLIATELLE: Dust sheets with flour and roll up loosely. With a sharp knife, cut into ½ inch ribbons. For papardelle, cut into ⅝ inch ribbons. For fettuccine, cut into ½ inch ribbons. And for tagliarini, cut into ⅛ inch ribbons.

FOR LASAGNE: Cut dough sheets into large rectangles or squares, depending on the size of your casserole dish.

FOR FARFALLE: Shape the dough into little "butterflies;" squeeze together 1 by 2 inch rectangles of dough in the middle with two fingers.

FOR ORECHIETTI: Shape dough into a thin roll, slice, and make a dent in each slice with your thumb.

1. Stir together ingredients.

2. Add flours to edges of well.

3. Add flour from center to combine to dough.

4. Knead dough until smooth.

5. Wrap dough in plastic wrap.

6. Roll out dough and cut into strips.

7. Run one piece of dough through widest setting.

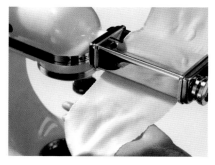

8. Run through two to three times for thin dough.

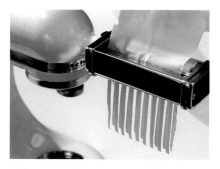

9. Use attachment on pasta maker for strips or ribbons.

Macaroni and Swordfish

1 lb swordfish steaks
2–3 tbs olive oil
¼ cup fennel, diced
¼ cup green onions, sliced
    into rings
2 cloves garlic, minced
1 red chile pepper, seeds
    removed and diced
16 oz diced tomatoes
12 oz macaroni
1 tbs chopped parsley for garnish
Kosher salt
Freshly ground pepper

CUT SWORDFISH into 1 inch cubes and season with salt and pepper. In a pan, heat oil and brown swordfish on all sides. Remove and set aside. In the same pan, add fennel, green onions, garlic, and chile pepper. Cook for 4–5 minutes. Add tomatoes and simmer for 20 minutes. Season to taste with salt and pepper. Add swordfish and simmer for another 5 minutes.

COOK MACARONI in boiling, salted water according to package directions until al dente and drain.

TO SERVE: Divide macaroni onto plates, top with swordfish-tomato sauce, and sprinkle with parsley.

Pipe Rigate with Vegetables

8 oz pipe rigate

½ cup heavy cream

½ cup vegetable stock

3½ oz smoked Scamorza
  mozzarella cheese, diced

⅔ cup cauliflower florets

2 tbs butter

2 tbs minced shallots

½ cup carrots, sliced

½ cup zucchini, sliced

½ red chile pepper, seeded
  and diced

½ cup yellow peppers, seeded
  and sliced into strips

Kosher salt

Freshly ground pepper

COOK PIPE RIGATE in boiling salted water until al dente, drain, and set aside.

IN A PAN, combine cream and vegetable stock. Bring to a boil, reduce heat, reduce by one-third, and season to taste with salt and pepper. Add cheese to the sauce and melt.

IN A LARGE POT, bring salted water to a boil. Add cauliflower and boil for 5 minutes. Drain and set aside. In a pan, melt butter and sauté shallots until translucent. Add carrots and cook for 3–4 minutes. Add zucchini and chile pepper and cook for another 3 minutes. Stir in cauliflower, bell peppers and cheese sauce, and simmer for an additional 3 minutes. Season to taste with salt and pepper.

PREHEAT OVEN TO 400°F. Fill a baking dish with pipe rigate and top with vegetables. Cover with foil and bake for 10 minutes.

Garganelli
con Formaggio

2 tbs olive oil
3 tbs green onions, chopped
    into rings
⅓ cup zucchini, sliced
⅓ cup red bell peppers, seeds
    removed and cut into strips
⅔ cup yellow tomatoes, diced
2 tbs butter
2 tbs minced white onions
⅓ cup heavy cream
4 oz fontina cheese, grated
12 oz penne pasta
4 oz Stilton
Kosher salt
Freshly ground pepper

IN A PAN, heat olive oil. Add onions, zucchini, bell peppers and tomatoes, and sauté over moderate heat for 4–5 minutes. Season to taste with salt and pepper.

IN A LARGE SAUCEPAN, melt butter and sauté onions until translucent. Add cream and melt fontina slowly over low heat while stirring with a wire whisk. Season to taste with salt and pepper.

COOK PENNE IN BOILING, salted water according to package directions until al dente and drain.

TO SERVE: Toss penne with the sauce. Cut Stilton into small cubes and sprinkle on top.

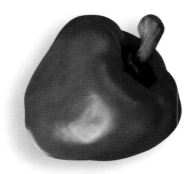

Penne with Ham

2 tbs butter
⅓ cup carrots, diced
¼ cup celery, diced
½ cup zucchini, diced
3½ oz cooked ham, diced
5 oz mortadella, diced
8 oz tomatoes, diced
⅔ cup white wine
16 oz penne pasta
6 basil leaves, chopped
    for garnish
¼ cup Parmigiano-
    Reggiano, grated
Kosher salt
Freshly ground pepper

IN A PAN, heat butter and sauté carrots, celery, and zucchini for 3–4 minutes. Add ham and mortadella and brown for 2–3 minutes. Add tomatoes and wine, and simmer for 10 minutes. Season to taste with salt and pepper.

COOK PENNE in boiling, salted water according to package directions until al dente and drain. Add to the pan and stir everything together.

TO SERVE: Divide evenly onto warm plates and garnish with basil and Parmigiano-Reggiano.

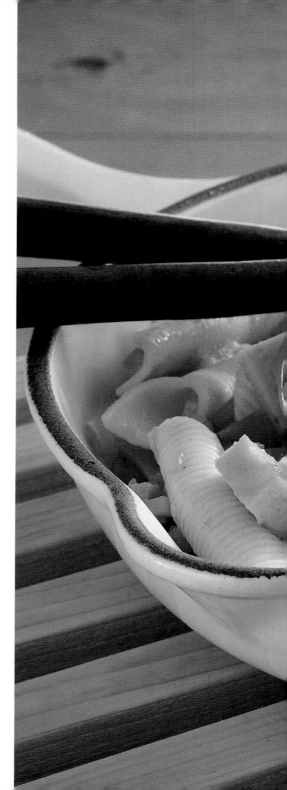

Seafood Rigatoni

16 oz rigatoni
1 lb squid
3 tbs olive oil, separated
⅓ cup onions, chopped
¾ cup dry sparkling
    wine, separated
8 oz tomatoes, diced
1 clove garlic, minced
1 small chile pepper, seeds
    removed and diced
1 tbs chopped parsley
20 medium prawns
Kosher salt
Freshly ground pepper

COOK RIGATONI in boiling, salted water according to package directions until al dente and drain. Set aside.

CLEAN SQUID and cut into rings and small cubes. In a pan, heat 2 tablespoons of oil and sauté onions until translucent. Add squid and sauté for 2–3 minutes. Add ½ cup of sparkling wine and tomatoes. Season with salt and pepper. Reduce heat and simmer for 10 minutes. Set aside.

IN A LARGER PAN, heat remaining oil and sauté garlic, chile pepper, and parsley for 1 minute. Add prawns and sauté for 3 minutes. Add remaining sparkling wine, stir, and add squid with sauce. Simmer 2–3 more minutes and add rigatoni. Season to taste with salt and pepper.

Penne di Estate

12 oz penne rigate
¼ cup olive oil, separated
4 tomatoes, diced
⅔ cup zucchini, sliced
4 basil leaves, chopped
1 tbs chopped thyme leaves
2½ oz pecorino, grated
Kosher salt
Freshly ground pepper

COOK PENNE in boiling, salted water according to package directions until al dente and drain. Set aside.

IN A SAUCEPAN, over medium heat, add 2 tablespoons of oil. Add tomatoes and zucchini, season with salt and pepper, and sauté for 2 minutes. Add penne and toss with remaining oil, basil, and thyme.

TO SERVE: Divide onto warm plates and sprinkle pecorino over the top of the penne.

Cavatappi from Madagascar

12 oz cavatappi pasta
¼ cup celery, chopped
¼ cup frozen peas
6 oz tomatoes, diced
1 vanilla bean, cut in half
   and pulp removed
1 tsp chopped marjoram
¼ cup pitted black olives, sliced
   into rings
⅔ cup cooked garbanzo
   beans, drained
¼ cup olive oil
Juice of ½ lemon
2 tbs shaved Parmigiano-Reggiano

COOK CAVATAPPI in boiling, salted water according to package directions until al dente. During the last 3 minutes, add celery and peas. Drain and cool completely. Set aside.

IN A BOWL, combine tomatoes, vanilla pulp, marjoram, olives, garbanzo beans, oil, lemon juice, and set aside pasta. Mix together and season with salt and pepper.

TO SERVE: Divide onto plates and sprinkle with Parmigiano-Reggiano.

Macaroni with Feta

¼ cup olive oil
½ cup onions, chopped
1 clove garlic, minced
1 small hot chile pepper, seeds
   removed and chopped
⅓ cup yellow zucchini, thinly sliced
¼ cup sun-dried tomatoes in oil,
   drained and cut into strips
15 oz tomatoes, diced
2 tbs small black olives, chopped
16 oz macaroni
5 oz feta cheese
1 tbs chopped basil for garnish
Kosher salt
Freshly ground pepper

IN A PAN, heat olive oil and sauté onions, garlic, and chile pepper. Add zucchini and sauté for 2 minutes. Add tomatoes and sauté for 2 minutes. Stir in olives and season to taste with salt and pepper.

COOK MACARONI in boiling, salted water according to package directions until al dente, drain, and combine in the pan with the sauce.

PREHEAT OVEN BROILER. Crumble feta over the top of the macaroni and brown in the pan under the broiler for 1–2 minutes.

TO SERVE: Divide onto warm plates and sprinkle with basil.

RIBBONS

FRESHLY MADE RIBBON PASTA is lighter and richer than its dried counterpart. The reason is that fresh pasta is made with eggs and dried uses just flour and water. Fresh pasta is typically found in Northern Italy, while dried pasta is typically found in Southern Italy. Both types are fine to use in the recipes found in this chapter. However, if you find yourself with a little extra time on your hands, give fresh pasta a try, you'll be glad you did. Otherwise, pull a bag out of the pantry and prepare one of these tasty sauces.

Fettuccine with Arugula Pesto

⅓ cup almonds, toasted
1 cup arugula, chopped
5 oz Pecorino Sardo, crumbled
3 cloves garlic, minced
1–1¼ cups extra virgin olive oil
8 oz fettuccine
Kosher salt
Freshly ground pepper

IN A FOOD PROCESSOR, combine almonds, arugula, pecorino, and garlic. Gradually add olive oil until it reaches desired consistency. Season with salt and pepper.

COOK FETTUCCINE in boiling, salted water until al dente (timing will vary depending on if you're using fresh or dry pasta) and drain.

TO SERVE: Toss fettuccine and pesto together, and divide onto warm plates.

Fettuccine with White Truffles

1¼ cups heavy cream
⅓ cup fontina cheese, grated
White truffles (amount as desired)
12 oz fettuccine
1 tsp chopped chives
Kosher salt
Freshly ground pepper

IN A SAUCEPAN, bring cream to a boil and reduce by half. Lower heat and melt cheese, stirring. Season to taste with salt and pepper.

JUST BEFORE SLICING, scrub truffles briefly under cold running water and dry immediately. Do not let them soak in water. Use a sharp, pointed knife to remove any dirty indentations. Do so sparingly as every gram is precious. Set aside.

COOK FETTUCCINE in boiling, salted water until al dente (timing will vary depending on if you're using fresh or dry pasta) and drain.

TO SERVE: Toss fettuccini and sauce together, transfer to warm plates, sprinkle with chives, and shave paper-thin slices of truffles over the top.

Tagliatelle
alla Rucola

3 tbs olive oil
2 tbs minced onions
1 clove garlic, minced
1 tbs finely chopped herbs
    (e.g., rosemary, basil,
    and/or parsley)
15 oz tomatoes, diced
½ cup arugula
8 oz tagliatelle
¼ cup Parmigiano-
    Reggiano, grated
Kosher salt
Freshly ground pepper

IN A PAN, heat oil and sauté onion and garlic until translucent. Add herbs and tomatoes. Sauté 5–6 minutes. Rinse arugula, remove hard stems, and cut leaves into small strips. Stir half the arugula into the sauce. Season to taste with salt and pepper.

COOK PASTA in boiling, salted water until al dente (timing will vary depending on if you're using fresh or dry pasta), drain, and combine with the sauce.

TO SERVE: Divide onto warm plates and sprinkle with remaining arugula and Parmigiano-Reggiano.

Tagliatelle
with Tomatoes

¼ cup olive oil
⅓ cup onions, chopped
1 clove garlic, minced
28 oz diced tomatoes
Pinch of sugar
1 small chile pepper, seeded
    and diced
12 oz tagliatelle
1 tbs chopped herbs (e.g., thyme,
    oregano, or parsley)
3 tbs black olives, chopped
Kosher salt
Freshly ground pepper

IN A SAUCEPAN, heat oil and sauté onions and garlic until translucent. Add tomatoes. Season with sugar, chile pepper, salt, and pepper. Simmer gently, uncovered, for 10 minutes.

COOK TAGLIATELLE in boiling, salted water until al dente (timing will vary depending on if you're using fresh or dry pasta) and drain.

ADD PASTA to the pan with the sauce, stir, and add herbs and olives.

Tagliatelle del Formaggio

2 tbs butter
3 tbs minced shallots
1 clove garlic, minced
2 small chile peppers, seeds
    removed and diced
1½ cups heavy cream
⅓ cup Emmenthaler, grated
3 tbs grated Parmigiano-Reggiano
8 oz tagliatelle
¼ cup blue cheese, crumbled
½ cup cherry tomatoes, cut in half
Kosher salt
Freshly ground pepper

IN A PAN, heat butter and sauté shallots and garlic until translucent. Add chile peppers and remove from heat.

IN A SEPARATE PAN, reduce cream by about one-third and gradually stir in Emmenthaler with a wire whisk so it melts slowly. Remove from heat, let cool slightly, and then stir in Parmigiano-Reggiano.

COOK TAGLIATELLE in boiling, salted water until al dente (timing will vary depending on if pasta is fresh or dry) and drain.

PREHEAT OVEN BROILER. Stir tagliatelle into the pan with cream sauce, top with tomatoes and blue cheese, and place under the broiler until the cheese starts to melt (about 1–2 minutes).

Tagliarini

with Clams

½ cup arugula
2 cloves garlic, 1 whole, 1 minced
¼ cup almonds
¼ cup grated Pecorino Romano
½ cup olive oil, separated
1 lb clams
12 oz tagliarini
Kosher salt
Freshly ground pepper

MAKE THE PESTO: In a food processor, purée arugula, 1 whole garlic clove, almonds, and pecorino, gradually adding ⅓ cup oil. Season to taste with salt and pepper. Set aside.

RINSE CLAMS, removing sand and barnacles. Discard any open clams because they might be spoiled. In a saucepan, heat remaining oil and sauté 1 minced garlic. Add clams, cover, and simmer for 6–8 minutes until all the clams have opened.

COOK TAGLIARINI in boiling, salted water until al dente (timing will vary depending on if pasta is fresh or dry) and drain.

TOSS PESTO AND TAGLIARINI together, add to the pan with clams, and season to taste with salt and pepper. Serve in warm bowls.

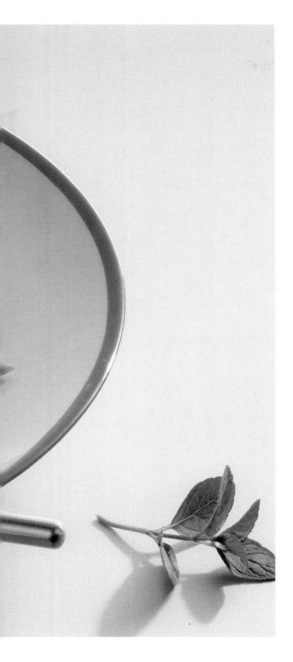

Pappardelle with Lemon and Asparagus

1 cup heavy cream
1 small chile pepper, seeds
    removed and diced
Juice from 1 lemon
12 oz pappardelle
3 tbs extra virgin olive oil
1 lb green asparagus, cut into
    3 inch pieces
4 cherry tomatoes, cut in half
4 thin lemon slices
Kosher salt
Freshly ground pepper

IN A SAUCEPAN, reduce cream by half and season with salt and pepper. Remove from heat. Add chile pepper and stir in lemon juice.

COOK PAPPARDELLE in boiling, salted water until al dente (timing will vary depending on if pasta is fresh or dry) and drain.

IN A PAN, heat olive oil and sauté asparagus for about 5 minutes. Add pappardelle to the pan and stir. Add cream sauce and toss gently. Season to taste with salt and pepper.

TO SERVE: Divide pasta onto plates, and top with tomatoes and lemon slices.

Pappardelle with Cherry Tomatoes and Chanterelles

16 oz whole tomatoes
3 tbs butter, separated
⅓ cup onions, chopped
4 oz bacon, diced
7 oz chanterelle mushrooms,
    cut in half
⅔ cup cherry tomatoes, cut in half
1 tbs chopped parsley
12 oz pappardelle
12 small sage leaves for garnish
Kosher salt
Freshly ground pepper

PUT TOMATOES THROUGH A STRAINER to obtain 1–1¼ cups tomato juice. In a saucepan, reduce tomato juice by one-fourth. Season to taste with salt and pepper, and set aside.

IN A PAN, heat 2 tablespoons butter and sauté onions and bacon for 2–3 minutes. Add chanterelles and sauté for 2 minutes. Add cherry tomatoes and sauté for 1 minute. Season with parsley, salt, and pepper.

COOK PAPPARDELLE in boiling, salted water until al dente (timing will vary depending on if pasta is fresh or dry) and drain.

ADD PASTA to tomatoes and mushrooms, pour tomato juice over the top, and toss carefully. Season to taste with salt and pepper.

IN A PAN, melt remaining butter and sauté sage leaves for 30 seconds.

TO SERVE: Transfer to warm plates and garnish with sage leaves.

Pappardelle
with Spinach

2–3 tbs olive oil
⅓ cup white onions, sliced
    into rings
2 cloves garlic, minced
¼ cup walnuts, chopped
16 oz chopped spinach
12 oz pappardelle
3 tbs grated Parmigiano-Reggiano
Kosher salt
Freshly ground pepper

IN A PAN, heat olive oil and sauté onions and garlic until translucent. Add walnuts and sauté briefly. Add spinach, cover, and sauté for 3–4 minutes. Season to taste with salt and pepper.

COOK PAPPARDELLE in boiling, salted water until al dente (timing will vary depending on if pasta is fresh or dry), drain, and toss in the pan with the greens. Season to taste with salt and pepper.

TO SERVE: Divide onto warm plates and sprinkle with Parmigiano-Reggiano.

GNOCCHI

GNOCCHI ARE LITTLE DUMPLINGS that are served as pasta. Basic gnocchi are made with russet or Idaho potatoes, but gnocchi can be made with many other ingredients such as cornmeal, spinach, and pumpkin, which are featured in recipes found in this section. As with other types of pasta, gnocchi are also best made from scratch. And, with a little practice, anyone can master the art of making gnocchi.

Cornmeal Gnocchi

1½ cups coarse cornmeal
½ cup Parmigiano-
    Reggiano, grated
½ cup butter, melted
⅔ cup heavy cream
1 tbs kosher salt

IN A TALL POT, bring 5 cups of water to a boil. Add salt and slowly sprinkle in cornmeal, stirring with a wire whisk. Cook gently over low heat for 45 minutes, stirring constantly with a wooden spoon.

PREHEAT OVEN TO 400°F. Butter a casserole dish. Using a tablespoon and repeatedly dipping it into cold water, scoop gnocchi balls out of the cornmeal and place in the casserole dish. Sprinkle the first layer of gnocchi with Parmigiano-Reggiano. Pour melted butter onto the second layer and pour cream onto the third layer. Bake in the oven until golden, about 10 minutes.

Gnocchi dei Frutti di Mare

Basic Potato Gnocchi (recipe
on page 109)
⅓ lb small calamari, cleaned
1 lb clams
¼ lb peeled shrimp
3 tbs olive oil
1 clove garlic, minced
2 tbs green onions, cut into rings
¼ cup carrots, peeled and diced
¼ cup celery
1 red chile pepper, seeds removed
and diced
⅓ cup dry white wine
1 tsp chopped basil
1 tsp chopped thyme
1 tbs capers
Kosher salt
Freshly ground pepper

CUT SQUID into small pieces. Scrub clams under cold running water, discarding any that are open, as they might be spoiled. Rinse shrimp and pat dry.

IN A SAUCEPAN, heat oil and sauté garlic and onions until translucent. Add carrots, celery and chile pepper, and sauté for 3 minutes. Add wine, clams and squid, and season with salt and pepper, cover, and cook for about 5 minutes. Discard clams that do not open. Add shrimp, basil, thyme and capers, and simmer uncovered for about 5 minutes, reducing slightly.

ADD GNOCCHI to the pan, toss gently, and season to taste with salt and pepper.

Gnocchi with Bacon

Basic Potato gnocchi (recipe
    on page 109)
7 oz bacon
⅓ cup hazelnuts, chopped
1¼ cups heavy cream
¼ lb radicchio, cut into strips
3 tbs grated Parmigiano-Reggiano
Kosher salt
Freshly ground pepper

CUT BACON into thin strips and fry in a pan until crispy. Remove bacon and drain on paper towels, setting aside grease for use in same pan. In the same pan, roast hazelnuts in 1 teaspoon bacon grease for 1 minute, stirring. Add cream and reduce by one-third. Add bacon and season to taste with salt and pepper, reducing slightly. Toss gnocchi together with sauce.

TO SERVE: Divide gnocchi onto warm plates, top with radicchio, and Parmigiano-Reggiano.

Pumpkin Gnocchi

½ lb russet potatoes
16 oz canned pumpkin
⅔ cup white flour
½ tsp kosher salt
¼ tsp freshly ground pepper
Pinch of nutmeg
⅓ cup heavy cream
2 tbs grated Parmigiano-Reggiano
2 tbs butter
10 medium sage leaves

PREHEAT OVEN TO 400°F. Rinse potatoes, wrap in aluminum foil, and bake for 1 hour. Peel potatoes and put through a ricer while hot. In a bowl, combine potatoes, pumpkin, flour, salt, pepper, and nutmeg to form a smooth dough.

ROLL DOUGH into 2 sausage-shaped cylinders ¾ inch in diameter, dust with flour, and cut into pieces ½ inch long. Roll the pieces over a grater to mark them with a grid pattern.

IN BATCHES, place gnocchi in boiling, salted water, reduce heat, and simmer. As soon as they rise to the surface, (about 5–6 minutes), remove, drain, and arrange in a buttered casserole dish so they overlap slightly and are almost standing on end.

POUR CREAM over the top and sprinkle with Parmigiano-Reggiano. Bake for 20 minutes.

IN A PAN, melt butter, and briefly sauté sage leaves. Remove sage leaves and set aside.

TO SERVE: Pour butter over the gnocchi and garnish with sautéed sage leaves.

MAKES 40 GNOCCHI

Basic Potato Gnocchi

1⅓ lb russet potatoes
½ cup flour
1 egg yolk
½ tsp kosher salt
Pinch of grated nutmeg

PREHEAT OVEN TO 400°F. Rinse potatoes, bake for 1 hour, and peel.

HEAP FLOUR on a work surface and form a well in the center. Add egg yolk, salt, and nutmeg into the center of the well. Put hot potatoes through a ricer and arrange around the top of the flour. Quickly knead into a smooth dough and let stand for 10–15 minutes.

ROLL DOUGH into 2 sausage-shaped cylinders ¾ inch in diameter, dust with flour, and cut into pieces ½ inch long. Roll the pieces over a grater to mark them with a grid pattern.

IN BATCHES, place gnocchi in boiling, salted water, reduce heat, and simmer. As soon as they rise to the surface, remove, drain, and keep warm.

MAKES ABOUT 96 GNOCCHI

Canederli

1 loaf (16 oz) stale white bread
4 cups milk
1 shallot, chopped
2 tsp chopped chervil
1 tbs chopped thyme
Pinch of grated nutmeg
½ tsp kosher salt
¼ tsp freshly ground pepper
4 eggs, whisked
8 cups beef stock
½ cup butter
¼ cup Parmigiano-Reggiano,
    freshly grated
Kosher salt

REMOVE CRUST FROM BREAD, dice into small pieces, and mix with milk. Soak for 30 minutes then squeeze out milk. In a bowl, combine bread, shallot, chervil, thyme, nutmeg, salt, and pepper. In a bowl, whisk eggs with a little salt. Add eggs to the bread and knead with your hands until all the ingredients are thoroughly combined and form a dough.

IN A LARGE POT, bring beef stock to a boil. Using a tablespoon, shape dough into balls and place in the stock.

AS SOON AS THE STOCK RETURNS TO A BOIL, reduce heat, cover, and simmer for about 10 minutes until the gnocchi are thick and round. Using a slotted spoon, transfer one at a time to a serving dish and keep warm.

BROWN BUTTER in a small pan, pour over gnocchi, sprinkle with Parmigiano-Reggiano, and serve immediately.

MAKES ABOUT 50–60 GNOCCHI

Spinach Dumplings

1 cup stale white bread
⅓ cup milk
1 lb spinach, chopped
2 eggs
⅓ cup flour
½ tsp kosher salt
¼ tsp freshly ground pepper
Pinch of freshly grated nutmeg
¼ cup butter, melted
2 tbs pine nuts, toasted
¼ cup Parmigiano-Reggiano,
    freshly grated

REMOVE CRUST FROM BREAD, dice, and mix with milk. Combine bread with spinach, eggs, flour, salt, pepper, and nutmeg to form a dough. Using a tablespoon, shape dough into egg-sized dumplings on the palm of your wet hand. Place in boiling, salted water, reduce heat to simmer, and cook for 5–7 minutes. Remove, drain, and keep warm.

POUR BUTTER into a casserole dish, spreading evenly over the bottom. Add dumplings, basting with the melted butter, sprinkle dumplings with pine nuts, and Parmigiano-Reggiano.

Cheese Dumplings

1 cup stale white bread
¾ cup milk
½ cup butter, separated
8 oz Emmenthaler or Swiss
    cheese, cubed
1 medium onion, chopped
1 tbs flour
2 eggs
1 egg yolk
2 tbs chopped parsley
½ tsp kosher salt
¼ tsp freshly ground pepper
Pinch of nutmeg
¼ cup Parmigiano-
    Reggiano, grated

REMOVE CRUST FROM BREAD, dice into small pieces, and mix with milk. In a pan, melt 1 tablespoon of butter, and sauté onions until translucent. In a bowl, combine cheese, onion, flour, eggs, egg yolk, parsley, salt, pepper, and nutmeg with the bread to form a dough.

USING A TABLESPOON, shape dough into egg-sized dumplings on the palm of your wet hand. Cook in boiling, salted water for 12–15 minutes. Remove, drain, and transfer to a serving dish.

BROWN REMAINING BUTTER, drizzle over the top, and sprinkle with Parmigiano-Reggiano.

PASTA GLOSSARY

ALPHABET PASTINI: These little alphabet letters make soup fun for kids of all ages. Letters from A–Z and numbers from 1–9.

BUCATONI: Long, like spaghetti, and hollow, like straws, these pasta strings are best accompanied with creamy Alfredo or medium-bodied tomato sauces.

CANNELLONI: Large round tubes ready to be stuffed with your favorite filling, then baked and polished off with a sauce. Cannelloni tubes can be purchased dry or, are unforgettable homemade.

CAPELLI D'ANGELO ("Angel Hair"): Long, fine, delicate strands of pasta create divine light dishes. Drizzle with a fruity olive oil or thin tomato sauce, or break them in pieces and add to soup.

CAVATAPPI ("Corkscrew"): These short, thin, ridged pastas look like twisted macaroni. Serve them with moderately thick and chunky sauces bake them into a casserole, or add some flair to a chilled pasta salad.

CONCHIGLIE: Shaped like conch shells, conchiglie and the larger conchiglioni are quite versatile. Stuff conchiglioni with your favorite filling, bake, and then drizzle with sauce. The smaller version will go in soup, salads, or with medium to thick sauces.

FETTUCCINE: With Roman origins, these "little ribbons" are thin, flat, egg noodles. Best known for their starring role in the, classic Fettuccine Alfredo, fettuccine is equally satisfying with a little olive oil, grated Parmigiano-Reggiano and chopped parsley.

GARGANELLI: A handmade rustic feeling sets garganelli apart from its cousin, penne rigate. The fine ridges and tubular shape provide an elegant spine to a smooth and rich cream sauce.

LASAGNE: Wide, and with rippled edges, there is no mistaking the lasagna noodle which lays the foundation for a baked lasagna casserole. Newer versions are thinner and don't require advance cooking.

MACARONI: Highly recognized and versatile, these short, curved pastas come in a variety of different shapes and sizes. Best known for their starring role in "Macaroni and Cheese," macaroni also shines in pasta salads and soup.

PAPPARDELLE: "Pappare," literally means "to eat." And that's exactly what you'll want to do with this flat, long, wide, egg noodle. Handmade pappardelle is a typical Tuscan delight served with a hearty meat sauce.

PENNE AND PENNE RIGATE: Meaning "feathers" or "quills"
in Latin, these diagonally cut, tubular shaped pastas are very versatile. Penne Rigate have ridges, enabling a hearty meat sauce to stick especially well.

PIPE RIGATE: These little pipes were once macaroni with ridges that someone pinched off at one end. The shape enables sauce to seep inside as well as cling onto the outside. Hearty meat sauces go well with pipe rigate.

RIGATONI: Large, ridged tubes about 1½ inches long. Rigatoni's robust shape and size make them a consummate favorite with hearty cream and meat sauces full of chunky vegetables or meat.

SPAGHETTI: Appropriately named by the Italians, spaghetti or "string" pasta is the most popular pasta form. And no wonder, with its versatility, spaghetti dominates main dishes, salads, and soups, mixing well with light and hearty sauces.

TAGLIATELLE: Synonymous with fettuccine, the Northern Italians call these long, thin, flat egg noodles, tagliatelle. Substitute accordingly and just for fun, serve a Tagliatelle Alfredo at your next dinner party.

VERMICELLI: Thinner than spaghetti yet thicker than capellini, vermicelli, or, "worms" in Latin, can be considered the middle child of pasta strings. Sometimes misunderstood, and often seeking attention, vermicelli is best served with lighter cream, olive oil, or tomato sauces.

INDEX